David Starr Jordan

Matka and Kotik

a Tale of the Mist-Islands

David Starr Jordan

Matka and Kotik
a Tale of the Mist-Islands

ISBN/EAN: 9783744714266

Printed in Europe, USA, Canada, Australia, Japan

Cover: Foto ©Thomas Meinert / pixelio.de

More available books at **www.hansebooks.com**

MATKA AND KOTIK

A Tale of the Mist=Islands

BY

DAVID STARR JORDAN

President of Leland Stanford Jr. University, and of the California
Academy of Sciences; United States Commissioner in
Charge of Fur Seal Investigations.

SAN FRANCISCO
THE WHITAKER & RAY COMPANY
(INCORPORATED)
1903

To My Associates

of the

BERING SEA COMMISSIONS FOR 1896,

with Pleasant Memories of the

Twin Mist-Islands and

the Icy Sea.

———

D'ARCY WENTWORTH THOMPSON,

LEONHARD STEJNEGER,

FREDERIC AUGUSTUS LUCAS,

JAMES MELVILLE MACOUN,

JEFFERSON FRANKLIN MOSER,

GERALD EDWIN H. BARRETT-HAMILTON,

CHARLES HASKINS TOWNSEND,

GEORGE ARCHIBALD CLARK,

JOSEPH MURRAY,

ANDREW HALKETT.

PREFACE.

In the illustration of this little book, I am indebted to Assistant Secretary Charles S. Hamlin, of the United States Treasury, and to Hon. John J. Brice, United States Fish Commissioner, for the use of photographs taken, for the various Bering Sea Commissions, by Mr. Charles H. Townsend, Dr. Barton W. Evermann, Dr. Leonhard Stejneger, and Mr. N. B. Miller. For certain photographs taken by Mr. Harry Chichester, I am indebted to the courtesy of Mr. Joseph Stanley-Brown. The drawings showing the life of the beach-masters were made by Miss Chloe Frances Lesley, a student in Zoölogy in Leland Stanford Jr. University. By the courtesy of Prof. D'Arcy W. Thompson and Mr. James M. Macoun, I have used certain photographs taken by the Commissioners of. Great Britain and of Canada. To the author of " The Beaches of Lukannon," I gratefully make any acknowledgment the reader may deem proper.

DAVID STARR JORDAN.

Palo Alto, California,
        January 19, 1897.

LIST OF ILLUSTRATIONS.

PHOTOGRAPHS.

PAGE

Matka, ... *Frontispiece*
(The Reef Rookery, photograph by *Charles H. Townsend*, 1892)

"Blue with harebells and spring violets, to the black
Tolstoi Head," 15
(Tolstoi Head, seen across the mouth of the Salt Lagoon, from
Asascardano, Zapadni Head in the distance.)

"Old Atagh had come back with the rest," 17
(Palata Rookery, Medni Island, 1892, *B. W. Evermann.*)

"When he had roared, he sat down on the snow and
groaned," 18
(Lukanin Rookery, *C. H. Townsend.*)

"They slept on Zoltoi sands when they were bachelors," 19
(Zoltoi Sands, *C. H. Townsend.*)

"Pretending not to see Atagh any more," 20
(Zapadni of St. George.)

"They lounged about him in pretty attitudes," . . . 21
(Zoltoi Bluffs, *Harry Chichester.*)

"The silken-haired ones," 22
(Zoltoi Bluffs, *Harry Chichester.*)

"'Oh, what a beach-master he is!'" 25
(Vostochni, *N. B. Miller.*)

"It is always afternoon," 26
(Lukanin, *Harry Chichester.*)

"One sleeps much on the Mist-Islands," 29
(Polovina, *C. H. Townsend.*)

"Polsi, who watched from the rock above, began to
laugh," 32
(The Reef, *C. H. Townsend.*)

"Time for Kotik to learn to swim," 35
(Tolstoi Sands, *Harry Chichester.*)

" The twin Smoke-Islands which sputter day and night," 36
(New Bogoslof, 1892,—first rose from the sea Oct. 28, 1883.—
N. B. Miller.)

"Old Amogada, with the long teeth," 37
(From a mounted walrus, *Miss L. Bernie Gallaher.*)

The young beach-master had courted Matka, . . . 38
(The Reef, *C. H. Townsend.*)

"One day Matka came ashore." 39
(Polovina, *C. H Townsend.*)

Zoltoi Bay, ... 40
(*J. M. Macoun.*)

On Zoltoi Dunes, ... 42
(*J. M. Macoun.*)

"No more life and bustle on the cliffs," 44
(Driveway of Fur Seals, from Vodopad over the mountains of
Medni, *L Stejneger.*)

"Rollicking away, like the jolly old boys they were," . 45
(Palata, Medni Island, *B. W. Evermann.*)

"Polsi tried to look strong and brave," . . . 46
(Zoltoi Sands, *C. H. Townsend.*)

"Stayed at Tolstoi, till every one else was gone," . 47
(On Tolstoi Head, *C. H. Townsend.*)

"On Zoltoi Sands when they were off duty." . 48
(*J. M. Macoun.*)

"Atagh and Unga came back, rollicking and roaring,"   49
(Palata, Medni Island, *B. W. Evermann.*)

"When the great ice comes,"   50
(East Landing, near Kitovi, in May, *Dr. Otto Voss.*)

" As though a great city had risen from the sea,"   . .   51
(Zapadni of St. George, *C. H. Townsend.*)

"This is Shishaldin; there the Storm King has his
kitchen,"   52
(Shishaldin, *N. B. Miller.*)

"The white volcano steams and puffs,"   53
(Makushin and Cape Cheerful, Unalaska, *Harry Chichester.*)

"Ungeskelligh, which means the place for bachelors,"   54
(Zoltoi Sands, *N. B. Miller.*)

"To be driven along in a crowd,"   55
(Zoltoi Sands, *C. H. Townsend.*)

"Not pleasant to tell the story of Asascardano,"   . .   57
(Tolstoi Drive, *C. H. Townsend.*)

" The twin Storm-Islands in the thicker mist,"   . . .   58
(Sikatchuiskaya, Medni, *L. Stejneger.*)

"Full of the joy of the great sands and the sea,"   . .   59
(Zoltoi Sands, *C. H. Townsend.*)

" No rocks to hide under and they cannot get out of
the way,"   60
(Tolstoi Sands — Trampled Pups, *J. M. Macoun.*)

"Shuffled down to Zoltoi Sands and swam away,"   . .   61
(Zoltoi Sands, *C. H. Townsend.*)

"The hollowed-out cliffs of Zapalata,"   62
(Zapalata, Medni Island.)

"The great Smoke-Island has ceased to roar,"   . . .   64
(Old Bogoslof,— rose from the sea 1768— *N. B. Miller.*)

"The ships of the Pirate Kings," 66
(Unalaska Harbor — Seized Schooners, "Onward," "Carolina,"
"Thornton," and "Angel Dolly," *N. B. Miller.*)

"Swarm in the icy sea," 67
(Unalaska Bay — Sealing Fleet, *C. H. Townsend.*)

"Atagh was sleeping yet," 68
(Tolstoi Sands, *Harry Chichester.*)

"The cries of the little ones go up day and night," . 69
(Starving Pup — Zapadni of St. George, *D. W. Thompson* and
A. Marrett.)

———

PEN SKETCHES.

(*Chloe F. Lesley.*)

PAGE

"Calling across the surf day after day," 16

"The little chutchki birds sang loudly," 17

"The mightiest of all the beach-masters," 18

"Then Atagh knew that they must fight," . . 19

"The black-zoned rock-fish," 20

"Like spectres in the great rollers," 21

"Bit him in the throat till Atagh roared again," . . . 22

"Boys are so silly; they don't go into society," . . 23

"I knew Matka before Kotik was born," 24

Isogh, the hair seal, ... 25

"But he never looked back to see how she fell," . . 26

"When Atagh was fighting, Matka would lift Kotik
gently," 28

"Matka never seemed to look at Kotik either," . . . 29

"'I do not like you,' said Kotik," 30

"Don't you see what heavy responsibilities I have?" . 33
(Zoltoi Bluffs, from a photograph by *Harry Chichester.*)

"The yellow Atka-fish with the black zones," . . . 35

"The purple squid, which tastes like peaches and
cream," 36
(From a specimen thrown on deck of the "Bobrik" in a
storm off Komandorski.)

"Rising and falling with the waves," 37

"A long ribbon of kelp in his teeth," 38

"Tumbling them over the cliff till the right one
reached her," 39

"Kotik went over with a splash," 40

Eichkao, the blue fox, ... 41

"And then he learned the dolphin leap," 42

"Old Sivutch himself was disturbed, and roared sleepily," 44
(Tolstoi Point, St. George — Young Male Sea-lions — from a
photograph by *Harry Chichester.*)

The pollock-fish, ... 45

"Orca, the Great Killer," 49

"Under the crest of a breaking wave," 54

"Old Epatka, the sea-parrot," 63

"Dead on the shining sands they call Zoltoi, the
golden," 64

"Gavarushka tried to take her eyes," 65

"'The decks of the schooners, smeared with their milk
      and their blood," 66

"'To the islands of the Four Mountains they have found
      their way," 67

"The dreary days have come," 67

St. Paul Island, Pribilof Group, Bering Sea, Alaska, . 71
            (After *Joseph Stanley-Brown*)

PERSONÆ.

ATAGH, a beach-master, homing on Tolstoi Mys.

MATKA, his wife.

KOTIK, their child.

UNGA, Atagh's brother.

POLSI (short for Polusikatch), Matka's brother.

HOLOSTIAK, Kotik's elder brother.

MINDA, Kotik's sister.

LAKUTHA, Kotik's sister.

ENNATHA, Matka's sister.

ANNAK, Ennatha's child.

IMNAK, a beach-master.

APOLLON BOWEDURFSKY, Chief of the Mist-Islands.

ISOGH, the hair seal.

AMOGADA, the walrus.

EICHKAO, the blue fox.

SIVUTCH, the gray sea-lion.

KAGUA, his wife.

CHIGNOTTO, the sea-otter.

BOBRIK, her son.

EPATKA, the sea-parrot.

CHUTCHKI, the least auk.

GAVARUSHKA, the burgomaster gull.

ORCA, the Great Killer.

Chorus of beach-masters, sea-lions, chutchki birds, volcanoes, southeasters, and surf of the sea.

"Blue with harebells and spring violets, to the black Tolstoi Head."

MATKA AND KOTIK.

Unsubstantial as a dream
Does my lone Mist-Island seem,
With its flower-bespangled moss,
Wet by wayward waves that toss
Flotsam from the farthest lands
Over Zoltoi's shining sands,
While the mist still broods above:
Sleep-cap of the Pribilof!

This is a true story, for I knew Matka before
Kotik was born, when she was very beautiful.
From the little window of the cabin in which I
write these words I can look across the salt
lagoon and the mossy hills of the Mist-Island,
blue with harebells and spring violets, to the
black Tolstoi Head where the great surf is breaking. Men call these cliffs *Tolstoi* — the strong one
— because they are so dark and heavy. Here,
among the broken columns of black basalt, was
Matka's home, and here Kotik was born.

Then, too, was I not with Apollon, the chief
of the Mist-Islands, when we found Matka dead

on Zoltoi sands, with the cruel spearhead fast
in her velvet neck? She had tried to come
ashore at Tolstoi, where Kotik watched her from
the rocks above, and little Lakutha waited on
the beach for her to come. But Matka was not
strong enough. The rocks were steep, the surf
ran high, and she had lost much blood. When
she tried to call back to Lakutha, the salt water
came into her wounded throat, and the tide rips
swept her away, over to Zoltoi, where the great
waves threw her body on the shining sands.
And little Lakutha waited for her on the flat
top of a broken column, close to the water's edge,
calling across the surf day after day. She is
waiting there yet, but she calls no longer, for she
fell asleep at last, and her little pinched body still
rests in the crevice between the columns of basalt.
But when Kotik was born, all this
had not happened. There was bustling
life on Tolstoi in those
days, when the ice
flocs all
melted in
the spring, and
the mist-lands above

"Calling across the surf day after day."

"Old Atagh had come back with the rest."

the rocks changed from white to green. The little chutchki birds sang loudly as they built their nests, and the whole shore was alive with the beach-masters and their families, returning to their homes from which the Storm King, who rules the twin Mist-Islands in the winter time, had driven them in the fall.

And in the spring, as it chanced, Old Atagh had come back with the rest. He had been far to the south, to the Fairweather grounds, where the black-zoned rock-fish lives, and he had chased it to its haunts among the granite boulders. He had come back strong and lusty, the mightiest of all those they called the beach-masters. When he blew his breath in a great, musk-scented cloud before his face, there were none who dared oppose him. When he had climbed over the ice floes

"The little chutchki birds sang loudly."

to Tolstoi, he roared, because the Storm King
had left one of his snow banks there. And
when he had roared, he sat down on the snow
and groaned, because he felt that great responsibilities were falling upon him. Then he roared
again, for by the rock at the end of the snow
bank, the same flat column   on which he
had stood all last sum-   mer, was his
own brother, Unga.   He knew
him by his thick,   brown hair,
his long mustaches,   and the scar

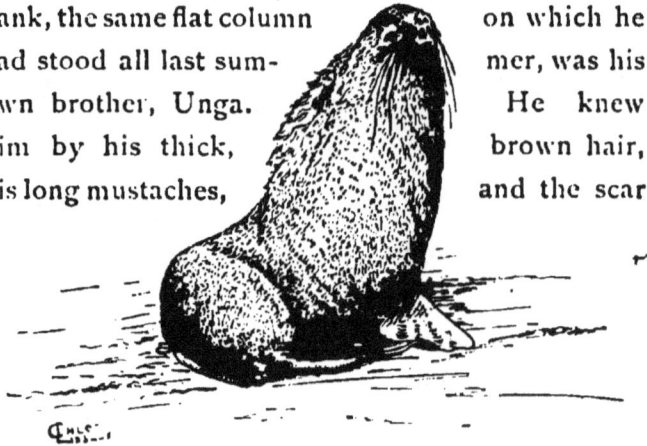

" The mightiest of all the beach-masters."

on his shoulder, which Atagh himself had cut
when Unga was paying court to Matka.

"Go away, Unga, I want that place," said
Atagh; and he groaned, and shook his head,
and sent his breath in a great, white cloud across
the snow. But Unga roared, too, and blew his
breath as far as Atagh could. Then Atagh knew

"When he had roared, he sat down on the snow and groaned."

"They slept on Zoltoi Sands when they were bachelors."

that they must fight; so he held himself very
low in the snow and struck out with all his
might, making a great cut on

"Then Atagh knew that they must fight."

Unga's arm just below the old scar, and the red
flesh showed again. And Unga stood up as high
as he could and cut the top of Atagh's head, so
that the scalp with its long, blonde hairs seemed
like a loose wig. Then Atagh rose as high as
Unga could, and seized him by the waist, and
with a mighty effort threw him from the snow.

Then they both groaned very loud, and the
big tears flowed from their eyes and made wet
strips across their cheeks, for they were sorry
that they must fight each other. For they were
brothers, and for many a day they had been great
friends. Long days and nights had they slept
side by side on Zoltoi sands. But this was when
they were bachelors, before the great duties of
life had come to them.

But the battle did not last long. When Atagh shook his blood-stained head, and roared again, and blew out his breath in a white cloud, Unga only opened his mouth very wide and looked toward the ocean, pretending not to see Atagh any more.

So they became good friends again, and Unga shuffled back to the other side of the snow and left Atagh by the rock he claimed as his own.

Then others came up and would have taken their places with them on the snow, but they could not. For Atagh would hold himself very low as he sprang at them, and Unga would stand very high, and before the intruders knew what

" The black-zoned rock-fish "

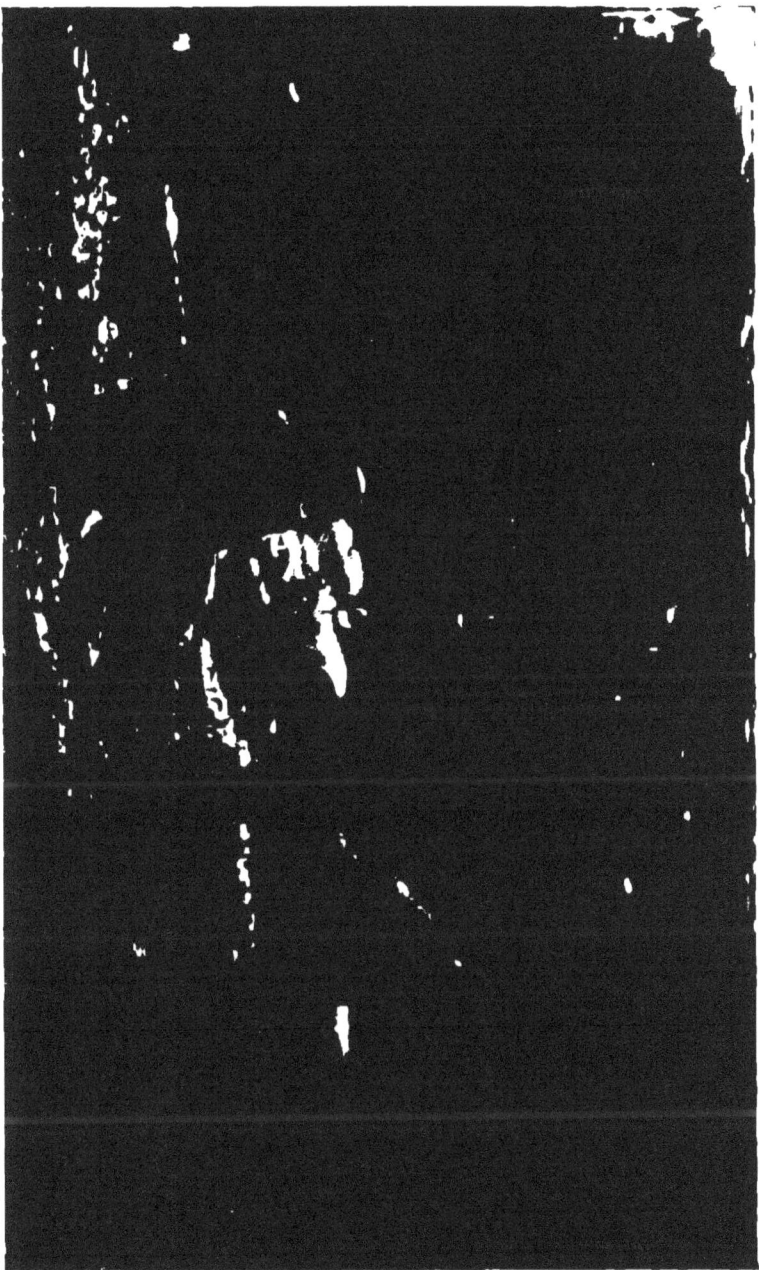

" Pretending not to see Alagh any more."

"They lounged about him in pretty attitudes."

had happened, they would be tumbled heels over head, down on the rocks of the beach. When they were all driven away, Atagh sat on the snow and roared again till the tears rolled down his cheeks, as he wondered whether Matka would never come.

One morning a long wave swept in from the sea, and there was a great bustle on the beach, a washing of faces and a shaking of rich furs,

" Like spectres in the great rollers."

and Atagh saw a dozen of the silken-haired ones climbing up the hill from the beach toward the snow where he and Unga were sitting.

But Atagh only groaned, and shook his head, and looked out toward the ocean, as if he did not see them. And the silken-haired ones saw his bleeding neck, and they said, "What a brave fellow he is; let us stay with him and give him consolation." And they lounged on the snow all about him in pretty attitudes, swaying back and forth their long, soft necks. Then they pulled his white mustaches and bit him in the throat, till Atagh groaned again and shook his head, and the tears flowed

"Bit him in the throat till Atagh roared again."

down his cheek, which meant that they were welcome. But none of them looked at Unga.

The next day there was another great rustle on the beach, for more of the silken-haired ones had come. And one of these was Matka, and Polsi, her brother, was with her. Polsi was talking to Matka very briskly. He told her about the Mist-Islands, and Ungeskelligh, and his little

"The silken-haired ones."

brown mustaches, and how he could almost blow a cloud, and how he would like to get married. And all the while the tears rolled down his cheeks. But Matka laughed. "O you boy," she said; "boys are always so silly; they don't go into society. One can't know boys, and you must never, never speak to me, for if you do, Atagh will blow a cloud at you, and you will feel no bigger than

"Boys are so silly; they don't go into society."

Eichkao, the little blue fox, for all your mustaches. Now, climb up on the parade ground, like a good little bachelor, and I will let you look down sometimes to see Atagh, that you may grow to be like him. Now, don't stand in my way, for there is Atagh waiting." Then Unga, who was all alone, groaned aloud, and

Polsi shuffled up the bank as fast as his legs could carry him.

So Matka shook out her silken-brown hair, and brushed her white throat, and climbed up the rocks to the great columns of lava. And Unga saw her as she came up, and stood in her way, and would not let her pass, for he was great and strong, and Matka was small and lissome. "Stay with me," said Unga; "I am all alone." Then he groaned very loud, and raised his neck, and shook his head three times, while the tears ran from his eyes. "See Atagh," he said; "he has enough already, and does not care for you at all."

"That is right," said Matka. "He is such a dear, good, masterful fellow; no wonder everybody likes him. We shall all have such good times together. Don't you remember how he threw you and old Imnak off the rocks last year, and carried Ennatha and all the rest of them to his own place, and you could

"I knew Matka before Kotik was born."

"'Oh, what a beach-master he is!'"

not help yourselves? How mad you were; but you could only groan, and could never blow a white cloud like Atagh. By the side of Atagh the rest of you beach-masters are no better than old white Isogh, who can't raise his head, and can only wriggle off into the water when a beach-

Isogh, the hair seal.

master looks at him. There were forty of us that year, and we all belonged to Atagh. Oh, what a beach-master he is!"

But Unga seized her by the throat and would not let her go. Then Atagh heard Matka calling, and he groaned and shook his head. Then, after he had groaned again, he rushed across the snow, and before Unga knew what had happened, there was another cut across his breast, through which the red blood showed again. And Atagh seized

Matka by the shoulders, and, feet in the air, he tossed her over his head so that she fell among the others. But he never looked back to see how she fell, and all the time he stood face to face with Unga, shaking his head and blowing out his breath in a great cloud. But Unga only looked out over the sea, as if nothing had happened. So the two were

" But he never looked back to see how she fell."

good friends again. There were now many more of the silken-haired ones on the shore, and some of them came to Atagh, and some of them to Unga; but I need not tell their stories, for it is always thus on the Mist-Islands.

So Atagh shuffled back to his place, and groaned as he thought of the responsibilities

"It is always afternoon."

of life. But Matka said briskly: "What a nice rock you have chosen, dear; and so many of them with you! How strong you are; how they all must admire you! There were forty last year; let us have fifty this year. But little brown Matka is the best of all; is n't she, dear?" And she snuggled up close to Atagh, and bit him a little in the sides of his neck, and pulled his long mustaches. And Atagh shook his head and pretended to groan, and the tears ran from his eyes, but he was pleased for all that, though he would never let Matka know it.

And Polsi, Matka's brother, watched them from the rock above the snow, and he shook his head and blew his breath out a little, just as he had seen Atagh do. But when Atagh saw him and groaned once, Polsi fell off from the rock and tumbled heels over head into the sea.

And right here, close to the sea, among the big rocks under Tolstoi Head, where you look down from the old fox-walk, Kotik was born. When I first saw Kotik the snow bank had melted away. The silken-haired ones were all come, and the Storm King had fled to his fastness in the north. Matka slept on the flat blocks of lava,

and Kotik was already a sturdy fellow, for Matka
had watched him closely all these first days.
None of the other silken-haired ones dared snap
at him when Matka was looking; and when
Atagh was fighting, Matka would lift Kotik gently
by the neck and place him in a safe place behind
some rock. Kotik soon learned to toddle away
and hide under the rocks when Atagh was rushing

"When Atagh was fighting, Matka would lift Kotik gently."

about, for to learn to creep under a rock so as not
to be trodden under foot is the first rule of the
Mist-Islands; and the second rule is, to go away
and play with one's fellows when one is not
wanted at home. Kotik had learned to know
Matka's voice, and to come when she wanted
him. He could climb the sides of the slanting
rocks all by himself when there was not anything
for him to eat. Atagh never looked at him, for

"One sleeps much on the Mist Islands."

he would not have Matka think that he cared for children.

Besides, as the summer went on, the responsibilities of life grew heavier on Atagh. He slept a good deal, and when he was awake he would shake his head and groan. And after a while, Matka never seemed to look at Kotik, either. But when he was out of sight, he was always in her thoughts; she would open her sleepy eyes, and without rising from her resting-place, she would call, and call, until Kotik should answer. Then she would go back to sleep again, and Kotik slept by her side. For one sleeps much on the Mist-Islands. The time moves slowly there, for it is always afternoon, and those who stay there sleep, and sleep, and wait.

"Matka never seemed to look at Kotik, either."

One day I came to Tolstoi Head, and looking down over the ledge, I saw them all fast asleep — Atagh beside his rock with his nose in the air, while Matka was lazily comfortable on her back among the stones, her arms spread wide apart and her white throat showing soft like velvet. Kotik lay close by her with outstretched limbs, trying to look as much like Matka as he could.

"O Matka," said I, "let me look at your little boy!" Matka woke with a start, and brushed her throat nervously with her hands. "Yes, you may," said she; "but I must go and wash my face." But Kotik said: "No, you cannot look at me. I do not like you; go away and let me alone. If you don't go, I will bite you, and I will tell Atagh, my father, and he will groan at you and bite you, too. Let me alone," said Kotik.

So Matka went off to wash her face in the sea. But Atagh saw her going, and would not have it. He groaned again over the troubles of life, and

"'I do not like you,' said Kotik."

one could hear him a mile away. He leaned back on the rock when he roared, and opened his mouth wide, and the tears ran from his eyes. Then he groaned again and shook his head four times. But Matka would not have me see her till she had washed her face, and she tried again to run away. But Atagh said, "Matka, you shall not go; I have said so, and I must have my way." So he seized her by the neck and flung her over his shoulder back into her place. "Look at me," he said; "I never wash my face; I never eat; I never drink; I never waste my time in frivolity. I have stayed right here at home all these two months. I have worked hard, and you shall stay with me." And Matka sat very still behind the rock and looked at Atagh admiringly.

Then Atagh saw me, and he groaned and shook his head again. "Go away," he said; "don't you see how hard it is to manage a household? When visitors come, they break up family discipline." And Kotik sat on the rock and roared, too, in his little, high-pitched voice, shaking his black head till I could see his white teeth. "Don't you see how you trouble us," said he; "it is all that we can do to manage Matka, anyhow, even if you don't come meddling with our affairs."

Then Polsi, Matka's brother, who was sitting alone, watching from the rock above like a sentinel, began to laugh. But Atagh snorted at him, and he ran away as fast as his long, flat feet could carry him, and while he ran he tumbled over little Holostiak, and they both went flip-flap, bumping their noses against the rocks till they splashed into the sea.

But Matka meant to wash her face all the time, though she pretended not to care any more, and she sat quite still and craned her neck, looking at me all the while with sleepy, curious eyes. "Do go away," said Atagh; "don't you see what heavy responsibilities I have?" Then he began to pant, for he was stout and growing scant of breath, and he groaned again when he thought of all the cares life had brought him.

Then Kotik began to cry as loud as he could. But no one took any notice of him. So he wiped his eyes with his flat, brown hands and ran off to play with the other black-haired little fellows, each with a white spot under his ribs. They were crawling up a flat rock and sliding back every

"Polsi who watched from the rocks above, began to laugh."

"Don't you see what heavy responsibilities I have?"

time they got half way up. And when one of them would fall off from a rock and bump his nose, then all the others would climb to the same place and do the same thing. And Kotik saw them; so he went up to climb, and slide, and bump his nose with them. And he was climbing and sliding still when I went away.

And Matka washed her face after all, for Atagh went to sleep after he had groaned some more; and Matka slipped softly by him and went down to the sea. For she always had her own way at the end. This is why Atagh groaned so much and shook his head.

When I next came to Tolstoi, Atagh was lying on the rock fast asleep, sprawled out at full length, his head hanging off from one side of the rock, his long feet dropping down from the other. Matka had been away for a week, but she had already taught Atagh that she should always do as she pleased. She had run down one day to wash her face in the sea, and Atagh was so sleepy that he could not hold her back. When Unga tried to stop her, she struck him sharply on the chin, so that he was willing to let her go. For he, too, was very sleepy, and groaned to himself because

"Time for Kotik to learn to swim."

life on the Mist-Islands was so full of responsibilities. Then old Imnak saw Matka coming, and
he tried to seize her and hold her back. But
Matka was as deft as a cat, and slid behind him,
and plumped herself into the water just beside
her brother Polsi, and they both went off making
long, dolphin leaps. But Matka looked back once
to blow a kiss to old Atagh, who had just waked
up and who pretended not to notice it, while he
groaned and shook his head. And she called
to Kotik, who was climbing a great, slippery
rock, from which he could slide down plump
into a little pool of water. For it was time now
for Kotik to learn to swim.

Where Matka went, no one can tell, for it is
only the silken-haired ones that know the way to
the bank of sunken
mountains which is the
home of the yellow
Atka-fish with the
black zones, and of
the purple squid which

" The yellow Atka-fish with the black zones."

tastes like peaches and cream, and the sleek-
skinned dream-fish, which is the nicest of all.
There are many who have sought for this bank,

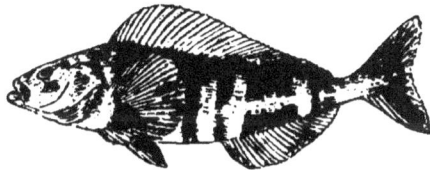

as there are many who have tried to find the
foot of the rainbow; but only the silken-haired
ones know the way, and those who have thought
that they found it have never been able to go
back to the place again. For it lies far away,
toward the Islands of the Four Moun-

" The purple squid, which tastes like peaches and cream."

tains, in the edge of the Icy Sea; and the giant
kelp spreads over it like a curtain, and rises
and falls with the rolling surge. To go there,
you must first find the twin Smoke-Islands,
which steam and sputter day and night, because
they are hot and the water they are in is
cold. Then you leave them well to the wind-
ward, and go on, and on, till you see Chignotto,
with the thick, gray fur, swimming on her back
in the kelp. Her little Bobrik she holds in her
arms, clasping him close to her breast when the
surf is high. And here the silken-haired ones

"The twin Smoke-Islands, which sputter day and night."
(New Bogoslof, 1892.—first rose from the sea Oct. 28, 1883.)

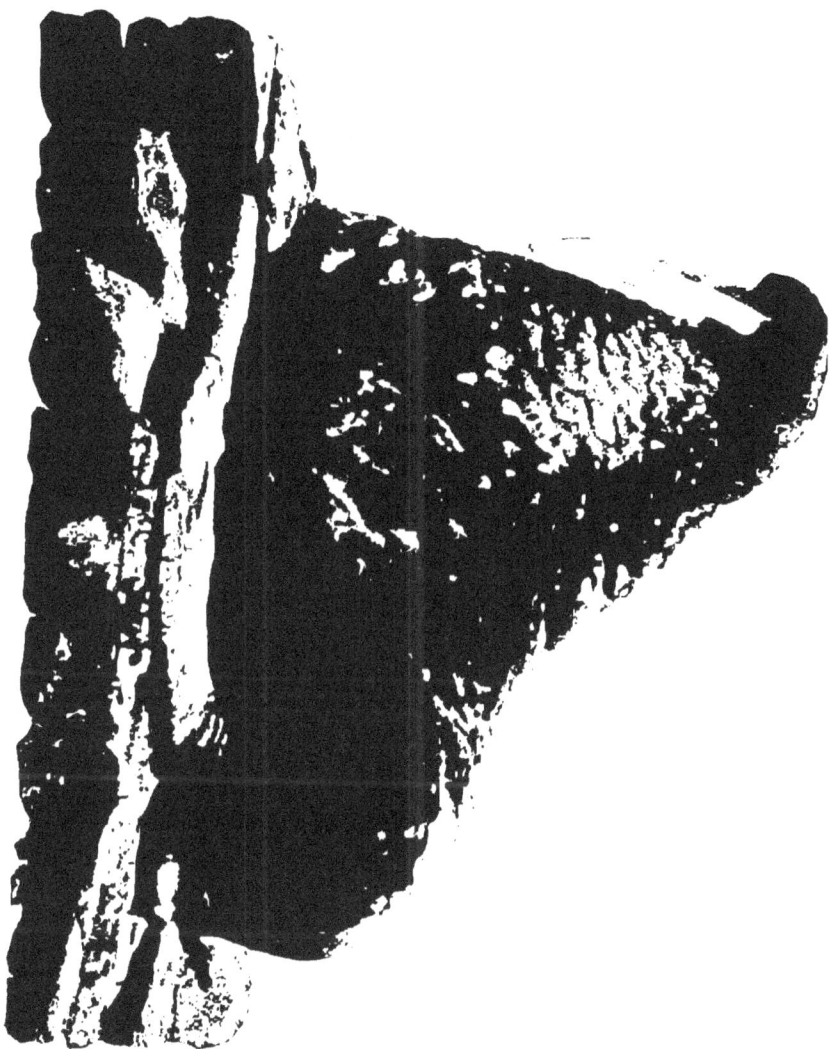

"Old Amogada, with the long teeth."

go when they are hungry, and they have no
fear of Chignotto, for little Bobrik claims her
whole attention, and all are friends who live in
the Icy Sea.

And there, too, is the home of old Amogada,
with the long teeth, who shakes his great head,
and roars, and looks very terrible. But Matka
had no fear of him, for she knew that he was
only scolding his wife, and whatever Amogada
says, she will do exactly as she pleases, for that
is the law of the Icy Sea.

When Matka had eaten her fill of Atka-fish,
dream-fish, and squid, she thought of hungry
Kotik, and of Atagh standing lonesome beside
his rock, with his nose in the air all these days.
But first, she must sleep a little, for a nap after
eating is always good for digestion, and she is
always well fed who   dines at the Sign

"Rising and falling with the waves."

of the Four Mountains. Besides, it is a rule of
the Mist-Islands that one should never go on
shore with fish in one's stomach. So Matka
lay quietly on the water for a day, rising and
falling with the waves, and when she awoke she
fanned herself softly in her own dainty fashion.

Atagh waited and slept, and when he was
awake he groaned and roared patiently. But
Kotik grew uneasy. He would slide on
the rocks, and paddle on
the water,
and sometimes
he and
his little
friends would
play beach-
master.

CHLOE LESLEY

He would seize a long ribbon of
kelp in his teeth and would shake

"A long ribbon of kelp in
his teeth"

his head very quickly, tearing it
to pieces, just as Atagh would tear the skin of
the young beach-masters when they came too
near Matka. And then he would pretend to
dive for fish, but he could only bring up a cast-
off shell or a piece of kelp. But whatever he

got he would shake with all his might so that it could not get away. And he learned to swallow the pebbles and shells, for one should always have a little of something solid in his stomach when he goes about on the land. Then he would try to talk to Atagh, but his father would only groan and act as if he did not see Kotik.

One day Matka came ashore. She shook out her hair, rubbed her eyes, and crept up the bank to her Tolstoi home. She looked neither to the left, nor to the right, pretended not to notice Atagh, who was sleepier than ever, and she called aloud, "Kotik, Kotik!" A dozen little black-haired fellows crept up the rocks when they heard her calling, but she thrust them carelessly aside, tumbling them over the cliff till the right one reached her at last. She gave him one kiss of recognition; but she would not even look at him after that, for she

"Tumbling them over the cliff till the right one reached her."

did not want Kotik to know that she cared
for him. So she made him wait until she
had dressed herself, and was ready to give
him his dinner, before she would turn her eyes
toward him again. For it is not good form
to show either love or anger on the Mist-
Islands.

When Matka was ready, she crowded Atagh
out of the way, and lay down on the smoothest
rock on Tolstoi, first pushing off all the little
ones who had gathered there to play, and had
gone to sleep before the game was finished. She
thrust them rudely down the bank, while their
mothers sleepily complained to Atagh. But
Atagh knew that Matka was always right. So
he groaned and shook his head, while she went
to sleep on the rocks, with Kotik by her side.

And when Kotik had taken all that she had
brought for him from the Sign of the Four

"Kotik went over with a splash."

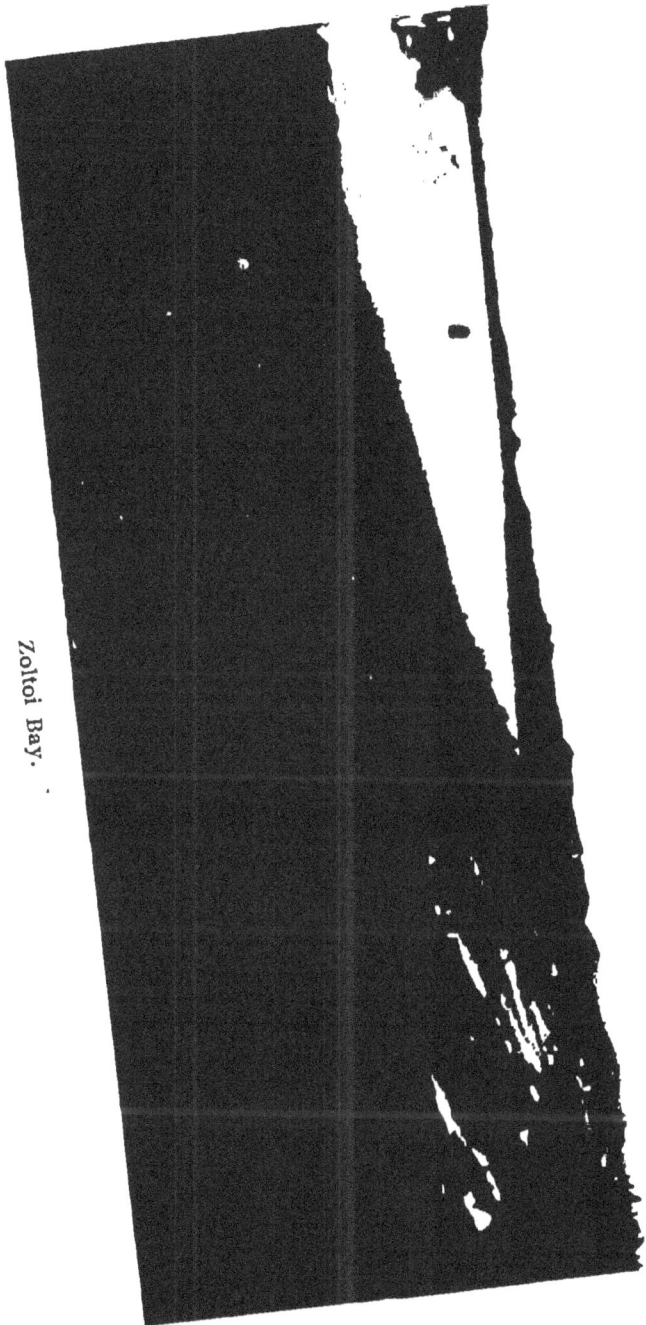
Zoltoi Bay.

Mountains, he lay down on his back under a rock, where no beach-master could step on him, and slept for a whole day, his flat, brown hands crossed on his breast, and his flappy little feet moving like a fan. And Atagh thought how pretty Matka was, and what a noble little fellow Kotik was coming to be. Then he leaned back, and shook his head three times, and groaned very

Eichkao, the blue fox.

loud. But that did not wake up Matka nor Kotik, for their sleep was all the sounder the more loudly he roared. "His voice is like the surf of the sea," Matka said, "and it does one good to hear it." Then Atagh laid his bushy head on the rock and stretched out his limbs just as far as they would reach. Soon he, too, was fast asleep.

One day little Holostiak was playing with Kotik by the water's edge, and for mischief he pushed the little fellow down the bank into the sea. Kotik went over with a splash. He was very much scared. He held up his head as high as he could, and then, before he knew it, his nose went under. Then he came up snorting and gasping, and if he had not paddled for dear life with both his flappy, brown hands, he would have gone to the bottom. Then he would have drowned, and the waves would have washed him up on the beach for Eichkao, the blue fox, to carry home to his children, as he had carried off little Annak the day before.

Then Holostiak showed him how to swim. He showed him that the way to keep his head up was to hold it low, so that only his nose was in the air, and to throw the water back with his hands. And then he learned the dolphin leap, when one swims partly under

"And then he learned the dolphin leap."

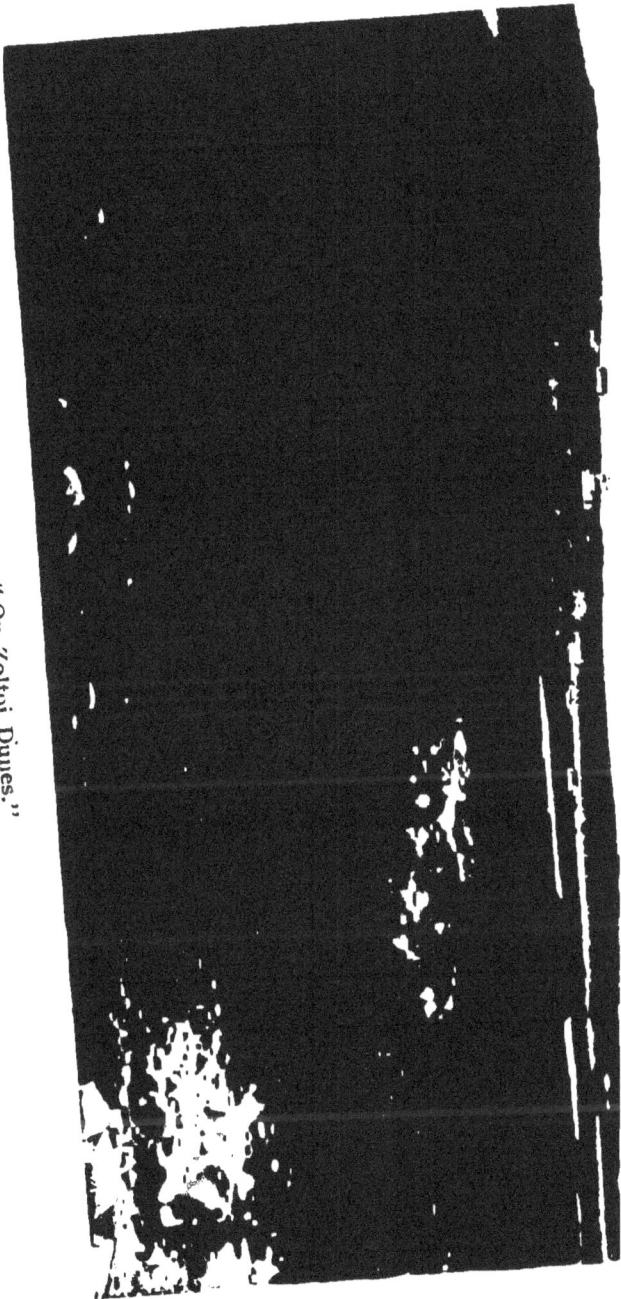

"On Zoltoi Dunes."

water and partly in the air, and breathes only when he is jumping. When Kotik could do this, he was very happy. And as he splashed about, the water washed away all his black hairs, leaving him all over a soft, silvery gray—"just like Atagh," he said in his little boyish pride. But Matka laughed, for she knew better. She knew that Kotik must shed his hair many times before it would be a full velvet brown, whitened by silvery bristles. Besides, Atagh had mustaches a foot long, and great teeth to bite with, instead of the little pin points around Kotik's mouth.

And when Kotik could swim very well, and could go all alone from Tolstoi to Zoltoi, Matka was very proud of him.

One day he swam around to the island where Sivutch, the gray sea-lion, lives, and he found the brown sea-lion babies asleep on the rocks off the shore. So he climbed up there with them, and began to play with them, just as he played with his fellows at Tolstoi. But the others said: "Go away, little boy. We can't play. We are big and all that, but we don't know anything. Let us alone." And they opened their mouths as wide

as they could, and cried, and cried, whenever
Kotik looked at them. And Kagua, the great,
foolish, white-skinned mother, plunged into the
water, and put out her head, and called piti-
fully in a deep, anxious voice, so that huge old
Sivutch himself was disturbed, and raised the
great mountain of flesh he called his
head, and roared sleepily. And
his voice was like the deep, full

"Old Sivutch himself was disturbed, and roared sleepily."

bass note of a mighty organ. You might go
around the world before you would hear the
like again. But Sivutch meant nothing when
he roared, for he was not even awake.

Then Kotik saw that he was not wanted by
the Sivutch family, so he swam away home and
found old Atagh groaning and shaking his head.
He said: "I have stood here on this rock all

"No more life and bustle on the cliffs."

" Rollicking away, like the jolly old boys they were."

summer and have not eaten once, nor washed
my face. You and Matka do not need me any
more. I am going away. Good-by. Take care
of yourselves. I will come back after dinner."
So, without any more ceremony, Atagh shuffled
down to the beach, not once looking back at
Matka. Unga followed him, and old Imnak
came, too, and they went off together in high
spirits, rollicking away like the jolly old boys
they were. For they were all great friends
always when they were off duty. And they
swam away together with great, dolphin leaps to
the Storm King's gate, where the pollock-fish
could always be found in plenty. For Atagh
was easily suited when he had enough to eat,
and he had no taste for the creamy squid and
the clear-skinned dream-fishes which the silken-
haired ones delight in.

The pollock-fish.

Then Polsi, who had sat alone on the rock above for a whole month, waiting for Atagh to leave, shuffled down to his place, and pulled his mustaches, and fanned himself unconcernedly, as he tried to look very strong and brave. He shook his head, and groaned, and blew out his breath in a little cloud. But whenever he heard any one coming, he trembled all over, and more than once he was scared out of his wits. Then he left the silken-haired ones and threw himself into the sea because he thought he heard Atagh growl.

But Polsi had good reason to be afraid, for one day Atagh came back all unexpectedly. He gave one great growl as he landed on the beach, and Unga, who was with him, roared and blew out his breath just as he had done .when they came for the first time. And when Polsi and the rest of them heard it, they put their heads low and shuffled off just as fast as they could. Then Atagh and Unga, who were very fat, and strong, and wide-awake, came back to their places rollicking and roaring, and they called the silken-haired ones around them, and everything went on just as before. When Matka saw

" Polsi tried to look strong and brave."

"Stayed at Tolstoi, till every one else was gone."

Atagh, she was very glad, but she pretended not to notice him. She was busy looking for Kotik, and did not stay very long in one place, and went from Atagh to Unga, and anywhere she pleased, just as Kotik did. And everybody began to do that, so that Atagh could not keep trace of his family. But he was rather glad to be free, and he went off one day to sleep on Tolstoi sands and get well ready for the Long Swim. Then Polsi, who had been watching all the time, came down and took his place. When the beach-masters are away comes the happiest time of all the year for those who are bachelors.

When Matka saw Polsi, she laughed. " So here the boys are coming to Tolstoi again. It is time for us to take the Long Swim, Kotik. See, the Mist-Islands are white and not green; the sun does not look at us any more, and soon the spray will all grow hard and slippery, and we cannot climb upon the rocks."

So Matka and Kotik swam off with dolphin leaps, and when they were well out at sea, they looked back and saw Polsi all alone on Atagh's rock. All of the silken-haired ones

had left him, and all their silvery-gray children
with them. There was no more life and bustle
on the cold, bleak Tolstoi cliffs. For Atagh
and Unga had already gone again. This time
they went to the Fairweather grounds, where
they would stay all winter, to come back early
in the spring. For they dared not go too far,
because they knew, that if they were not back
early, someone else would take their places, and
they might never get back into society again.

But Polsi stayed on Tolstoi till everyone
else was gone, and was very happy, because
he was now as good as Atagh. And little
Holostiak, who was Kotik's older brother, crept
down to Unga's place, and the Storm King
brought the snow back again, and the two
stood alone upon it, and felt very proud and
manly.

All at once Polsi said: "I feel very hungry.
Why, I have n't eaten a thing for a month.
Let us go and get some pollock-fish." "Just
what I was thinking of," says Holostiak; "they
can all see now that we are real beach-masters;
now the thing for us to do is to have a good
dinner." So they went down to the sea, and

On Zoltoi Sands when they were off duty.

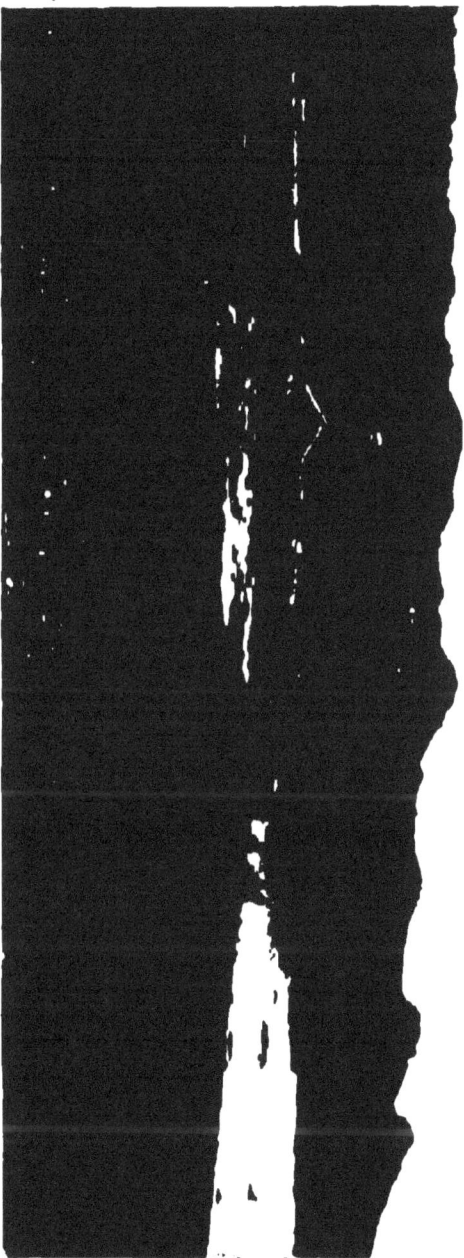

"Alagh and Unga came back, rollicking and roaring."

washed their faces, and then swam right away to the Storm King's gate, where the pollock lives, and is soft and tender. When they had eaten all they could, and had a long sleep on the waves, they swam across to the Fairweather grounds, where they found Atagh and Unga. But they were afraid of them no more, and they went on farther, and farther, a thousand miles to the south. They dodged the Great Killer, Orca, who would have stained the sea with their blood. For he hates the sons of the beach-masters, and destroys them whenever he can; and often he lies in wait for them as they pass through the Storm King's gate.

They passed Kotik and Matka, and all the rest of the silken-haired ones, till they came to the Gray-Islands in the Blue Seas. At the

" Orca, the Great Killer."

Gray-Islands the mist was all gone, the sunshine was hot, and they could see the moon overhead at night. Then they knew that it was time to go back. So they swam around all the islands, not forgetting the last one with the tall, ragged, brown cliffs, and the caves where the brown sea-wolves yelp day and night, in their silly, puppy fashion. Then they went straight back to the north, taking always the coldest current, going through the gates of the Storm King, and past the black cape, called Cheerful, and by the line of the great floes they found their way to the Icy Seas, to the Mist-Islands. And on the flat columns of Tolstoi Head, Polsi and Holostiak climbed first of all, and they found the snow bank there just as it was the year before.

When Unga and Atagh came back again and saw them, they blew out their breath in great white clouds. Holostiak ran away with all his might, but Polsi was not frightened at all. For he could roar and blow a cloud, and his teeth were long and sharp. So Atagh had the hardest fight of his. life before he could drive away Matka's brother. When the struggle was over,

" When the Great Ice comes."

"As though a great city had risen from the sea."

and each one had a bloody. shoulder, they were all good friends again, and pretended not to see each other. But there were three of them on the snow bank instead of two, and Polsi was in the middle, and could groan and shake his head just as well as Atagh could. When the silken-haired ones came back, it was very hard for them to choose, for, though Polsi's mustaches were not quite so long, his hair was very black, and he shook his head proudly, and could blow out his musky breath in great white clouds across the snow. And on Tolstoi again it was as though a great city had risen from the sea.

Matka and Kotik, too, had gone far out into the broad, blue sea, careless of storm or sunshine, so long as they moved on, day by day, in their southward course. They found many fishes on their way — white-fish and rose-fish, but the yellow Atka-fish of the Icy Sea tasted better than any. "Now," says Matka at last, " let us go back home." And they swam back strongly and swiftly, for Kotik was almost as large as his mother now, and his feet and hands were bigger. Every day, as they came nearer and nearer to the Mist-Islands, they grew

more and more merry. One morning, they saw
a great cone-shaped mountain with smoke coming
out of the top. "That is Shishaldin," said Matka;
"there the Storm King has his kitchen; from
that you will know your way home. Now you
see the thick mists rushing through the snow
mountains. That is Akutan and the gate of the
Storm King, through which you go to the Icy
Sea. Then you come to the great Moss-Island,
where the white volcano steams and puffs.
There the mountain is cleft in twain, and a white
cascade leaps from the midst of it straight out
into the sea. Now the gray mists draw their
curtain before the scorching sun. Where you
see the water falling, it is the Cape called
Cheerful, and you know you are almost home.
Two days more, and we will see the Mist-
Islands, and old Atagh waiting for me at
Tolstoi."

"Waiting for you, Matka," said Kotik; "cannot I go to Tolstoi, too?" "No, you foolish
boy," says Matka, "you must not come to
Tolstoi. Atagh would be very angry, and all
the silken-haired ones would bite you. You
must go off with Holostiak, and Kamnin, and

"This is Shishaldin; there the Storm King has his kitchen."

"The white volcano steams and puffs."

all the rest of them, to the sands of Ungeskelligh. There you may swim in the water every day, and you may sleep on the sands when it is warm, and on the grass when it is wet. And you may swim to Lukanin when the surf is high, and to Zoltoi when the wind is in the east; and you may swim and eat, and play and sleep, as you will. But you must never come to me. And when you swim past Tolstoi, you may call to me, but I shall never answer; and Atagh will groan and shake his head because you are such a foolish boy. And when the chief, Apollon, comes to drive you up, you must go right along and make no fuss, for it is the way on the Mist-Islands."

And Kotik was sad, for he wanted to stay with Matka. He loved the black rocks of Tolstoi, and he didn't want to be driven up. But then a great wave swept over the reef, and the silken-haired ones came up rustling and bustling to Tolstoi, and climbed over the rocks to where Atagh, and Polsi, and Unga were waiting, each with his nose in the air, and pretending not to see them. "Good-by," said Matka, and Atagh roared so loudly that Kotik was terribly

frightened, and swam away so hastily that he did
not stop till he reached the long, curving stretch
of sands beyond Tolstoi they called Ungeskelligh,
which means the place for bachelors.

Here he found Holostiak, and his mustaches
were growing, and he could already blow a
little cloud. And there were many more of

" Under the crest of a breaking wave."

the bachelors, little and big, and they had a
joyous time together. Sometimes they would
pretend to fight, to groan, and to blow out
their breath. But this was only play, for they
never hurt each other. Then they would bound
down the sands into the sea, and swim around
to Zoltoi and back again with long, dolphin
leaps. And they liked above all to creep
under the crest of a breaking wave, so that they

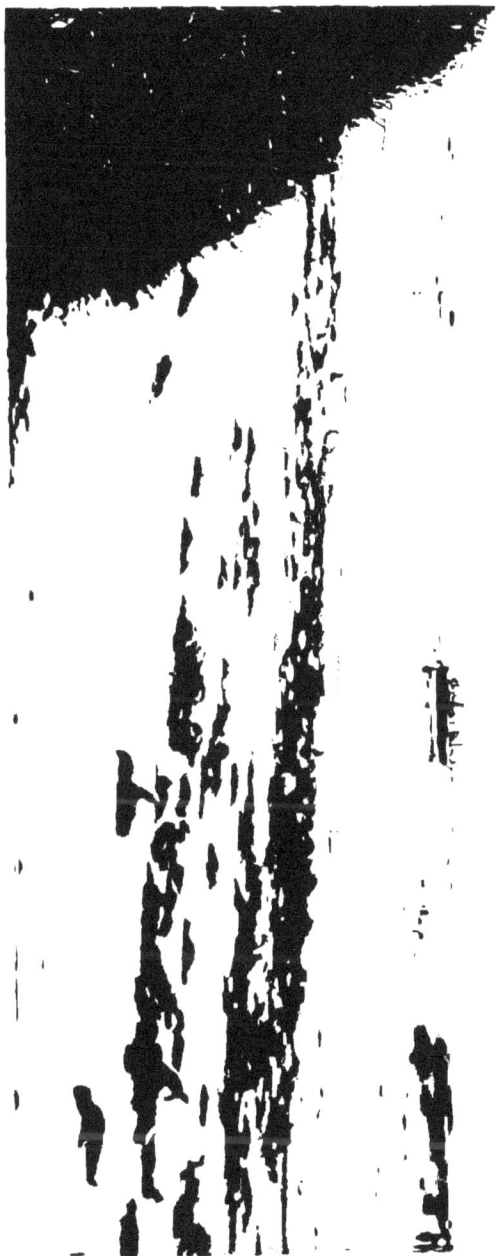

" Ungeskelligh, which means the 'place for bachelors.'"

"To be driven along in a crowd."

could look out on either side as it fell over them. And when he went around Tolstoi Head, Kotik would call out to Matka, and Atagh would shake his head at him and groan. But Matka was busy with little Minda, and she never answered back.

One night they were all asleep on the Unge-skelligh sands when they heard some one moving about in the mist. Holostiak awoke, sniffed, and raised his head. "That is Apollon," he said. "There is going to be a drive." Then he ran down to the sea and plunged in, and never stopped till he came to Tolstoi, so frightened was he. Here he climbed up the rocks and rushed right in among the silken-haired ones, scarcely knowing what he was doing. "The drive, the drive," he screamed. "What do you want here?" growled Polsi; and he and Unga seized Holostiak by the shoulders and threw him off from the rocks into the sea in half the time it takes to tell it. And Matka looked up sleepily and said: "Dear, dear, how foolish these boys are! I thought Holostiak had been killed in a drive by this time. I hope Kotik will never be so silly. I am glad that Minda is not a boy."

So the drive went on, and the bachelors were all awakened from their sleep, and men stood between them and the water, so that they had to climb up the sands and over the hill. It was hard work to go up hill in the sands, and they stepped on each other's feet, and tumbled about in confusion. But it was good fun for Kotik. Every minute something new would happen. Some of them would stop and shake their heads, snorting and groaning. Then Kotik would laugh at them and pretend to bite them in the throat or ribs.

When they came up from the sand over the rocks, they went along much more easily. And it was pleasant on the wet grass where the yellow poppies grow, and the great, blue violets. But Kotik did not care for these; he liked the cool dew, and it was such a joke to be driven along in a crowd. But when they came to go down hill, they would slip, and step on each other's feet, and roll heels over head in funny confusion. When they came to a little pond, they all plunged into it and made a great splashing.

The drive came to its end at the old killing ground, Asascardano, beside the salt lagoon, where the purple monk's-hood waves its poisoned

" Not pleasant to tell the story of Asascardano."

flowers, and the rye-grass is tall, because the bones lie thick about its roots. There were many others there from Lukanin and Zoltoi, and they all lay down in the grass, panting and pretending to bite each other.

Then Kotik saw a little "pod" of thirty, that the chief had driven up apart from the rest, and the men closed in about them in a moment, and only the biggest and smallest ones were left; for all those who were three years old, and whose skins had no scars, lay dead on the grass. It is not pleasant to tell the story of Asascardano. If killing must be done, one does not like to hear about it. So, if my lady wishes to know where her rich fur cloak comes from, she must ask some one else.

Kotik did not mind it much till his "pod" from Tolstoi was driven up. But when he saw the blows falling on his companions' heads, he was furious with wrath, and the big tears ran all over his face. He rushed at Apollon and struck at him with all his might, just as he had seen Atagh strike at old Unga. But the chief kept him off with his club, and Kotik could not reach him anywhere.

When the killing was over, and those who were left were creeping disconsolately through the grass on their way down to the salt lagoon, Kotik would not go. He groaned, and shook his head, and showed all his white teeth. "He's a fine fellow; hear him growl," said the chief. "When he grows up, then look out."

But the chief went away and left him. They drove up another pod a little way off, and Kotik was left in the grass all alone with his wrath. When he found that he could not get at the chief, Kotik shuffled off to the lagoon and swam back as straight as he could to Ungeskelligh sands. And he forgot to call to Matka as he went around Tolstoi Head, for his little heart was full of anger.

I should like, if I could, to tell how Kotik resolved that there should be no more drives, and how he led all the silken-haired ones and all the beach-masters in a great revolt, and swam away to the twin Storm-Islands in the thicker mist, where the green foam curls about the hollowed-out cliffs of Zapalata, and the black reefs close the way to all intruders. But

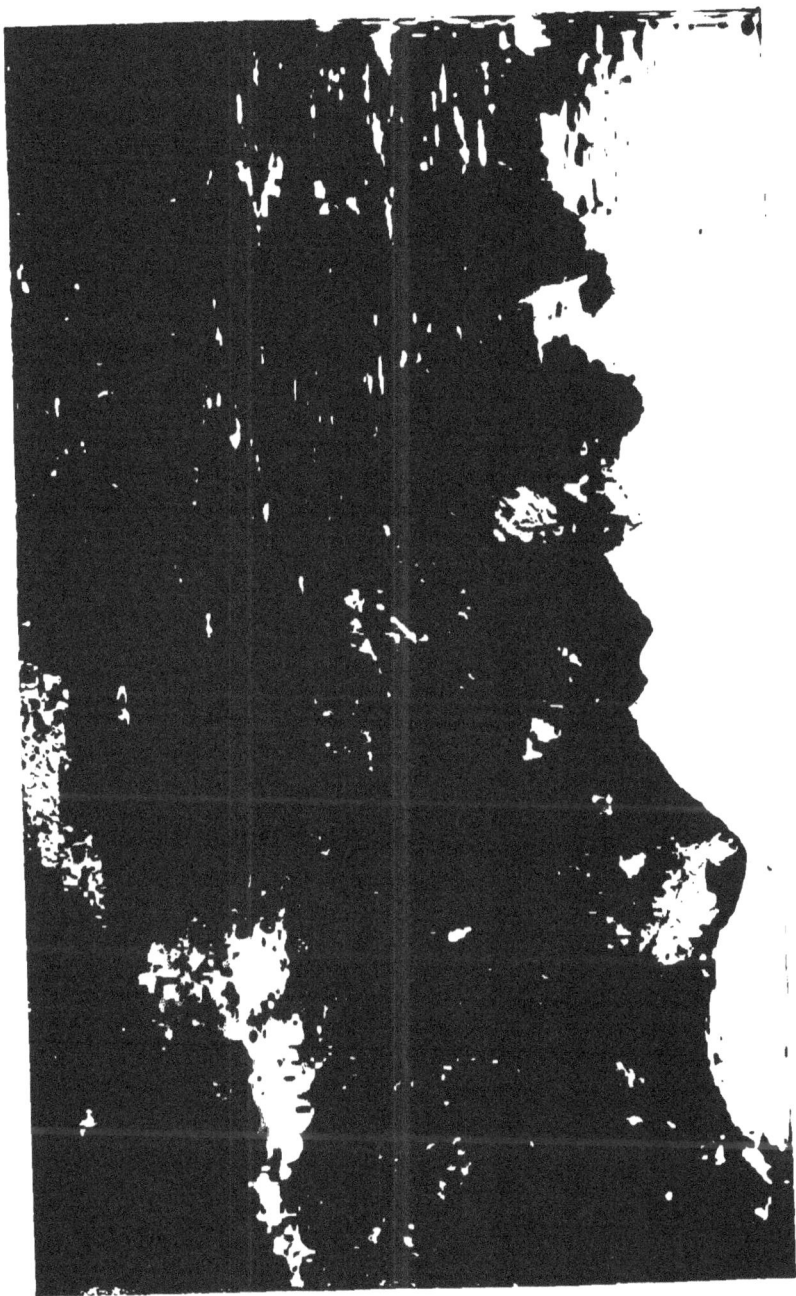

" The twin Storm-Islands in the thicker mist."

"Full of the joy of the great sands and the sea."

this is a true story, and I can tell only the truth. He did nothing of the kind. When he came to Ungeskelligh, Kotik found the strand so quiet and the sand so cool, the surf-beat so soothing and the mist so pleasant, that he lay down and went to sleep.

For it is the way of the Mist-Islands, that when one is unhappy he sleeps well, and when he awakes all is forgotten. Kotik awoke, full of the joy of the great sands and the sea, and his anger had all faded away. Ten days later, when Apollon came around again, Kotik followed in the drive, doing just what was expected of him from start to finish. And so did Holostiak, for he had less fear of the drive than of Atagh's terrible groan and Polsi's sharp teeth. "For there have always been drives," every one said, "and drives there will always be." And it is well for them that it is so, else the whole Mist-Islands would be covered with struggling beach-masters, and the silken-haired ones would have no peace of mind or body, and their little ones would all be trampled under foot. Even now, when the beach-masters fight on Tolstoi Sands, many little ones are killed, because there are no rocks to hide under, and they cannot get out of the way.

But Kotik did not forget Matka, and one day he went over to Tolstoi Head and climbed right up among the silken-haired ones, taking always good care to be on the other side of the rocks from Atagh. And Matka looked at him sleepily and said, "You foolish boy." But she did not drive him away. Atagh looked over at him and growled. But he knew it was only Kotik. Besides, Atagh was very sleepy. So he lay down and pretended not to see him. After a while, Matka said, "Now, be a good boy; go away, and when the Great Ice comes down from the north we will all swim off together."

So Kotik went down to the shore. Unga and Polsi growled at him all the way down, but no one did more than growl. On the shore he found little Minda, and he spent the whole afternoon teaching her to swim. Then he went around to Lukanin, for he liked to lie on the level rocks that face the long curve of the beach. The soft sand made his short legs tired, so when he wished to rest he climbed upon the rocks. But to the rocks of Tolstoi he

"Shuffled down to Zoltoi Sands, and swam away."

would not go again, for he would not be likely
to find Atagh another time in such gentle mood.

Holostiak and Kotik were good friends, and
went about together a good deal, climbing the
rocks or swimming about the Mist-Islands in
dolphin leaps, looking like spectres in the great
rollers.

But one day Holostiak stepped on Kotik's
foot. He did it on purpose, just to see the
little fellow sprawl on the sand. Then Kotik
growled and blew out his breath, and Holostiak
groaned and held his head low, striking Kotik
a quick blow on the shoulder. Then Kotik
raised his head, looking the other way, and pretended not to notice it. So they were good
friends again, and Kotik was very proud of
the scar, for it showed that he was big enough
to fight, even if Apollon had turned him off
four times from the drive.

When Unga and Atagh left Tolstoi again
and went off to sleep on the rocks, Holostiak
and Kotik climbed to the place where they
had been, and pretended to groan over the
responsibilities of life, to blow out their breath,
and to push about the silken-haired ones, just

as they had seen the beach-masters do. But the silken-haired ones only laughed at them, and said to their children, "It is time for us to be gone, for the boys are playing beach-master." But Matka waited to the last for Kotik, just as she had promised.

Then came another year, and Kotik had to go away again to Ungeskelligh with the others. But Apollon turned him back from every drive, because he was still too small. Holostiak would not stay on the sands any longer with Kotik. He climbed up over the rocks at Tolstoi, and sat there all summer long, looking down at Atagh and Polsi, just as Polsi had done the years before.

The next year Kotik was a splendid fellow, with skin as soft as Matka's, and his mustaches were plainly to be seen. He went into the drive again, and he thought himself the best of them, for he was now three years old. But Apollon turned him back just the same, because he had a scar on his shoulder, and would only make a second-grade skin at the best, for all he was so brave. And Kotik felt ashamed of his scar and himself. Then, whenever the time came

"The hollowed-out cliffs of Zapalata."

or the drive, and he heard the chief coming, he plunged right into the sea. So, when the others were driven, he was always out of reach, on the sands, or the cliffs, or the waves, so that he never went to Asascardano any more.

And the fourth year, and the fifth, he left the sands and watched all summer long on the rocks overlooking Tolstoi. Sometimes he stood on the cliffs, above his mother, like a sentinel, nose in the air. By his side, day and night, was old Epatka, the sea-parrot, who sits on one egg and never speaks, and who has no friends among the other birds. His bill is made of red sealing wax, and he covers his face with a white

"Old Epatka, the sea-parrot."

mask, so that no one knows what he is really like. He is a fantastic creature, and his temper is as bad as his looks, and he has many quarrels with the little blue fox, for the bones of his fathers lie bleaching by Eichkao's den.

But Kotik liked him, and Epatka did not fear Kotik, and they spent many days together on the rocks beside the old fox-walk.

Kotik's face was always turned toward Matka and Atagh. Sometimes he would climb up from below and stretch himself, like a great lizard, along the boulders over which the surf was breaking. But when Atagh would roar and blow out his breath, he would run away as fast as he could, plumping into the water with a great splash, and looking back at Matka by the sea.

And then at last came the sad summer, when the ships of the Pirate Kings found their way into the Icy Sea. It was then that we picked up Matka, with a spearhead in her throat, dead on the shining sands they call Zoltoi, the golden. And Lakutha, her little one, who had been so

" Dead on the shining sands they call Zoltoi, the golden."

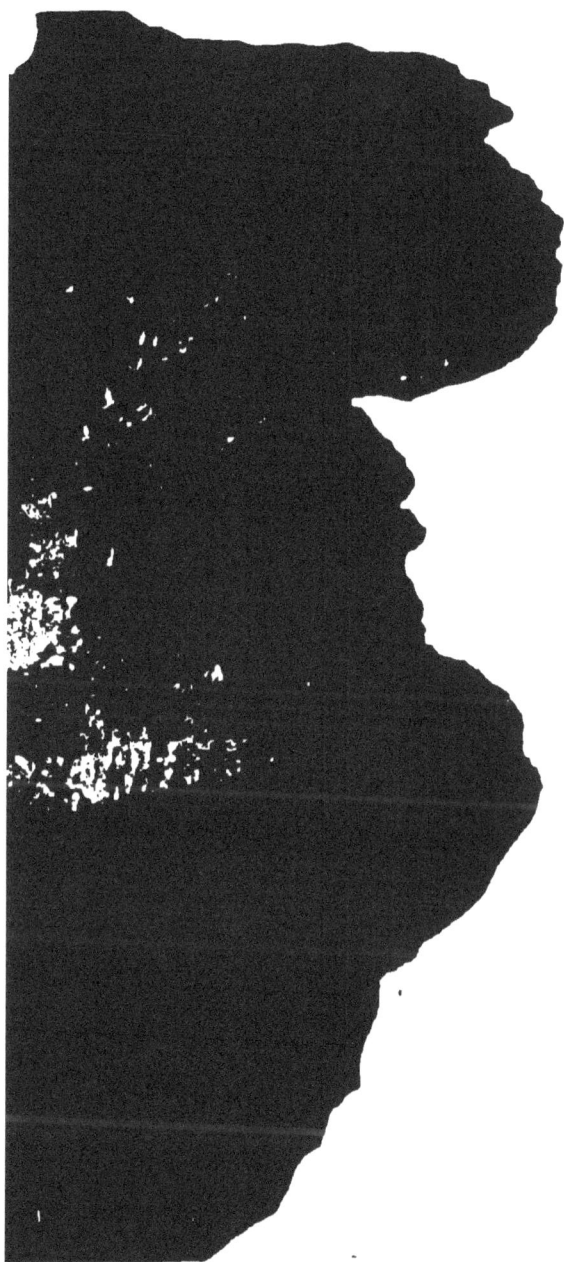

plump and joyous, grew faint and thin, until she died at last. Atagh was sore at heart, though he pretended not to notice it. But he groaned and shook his head with all his might when the blue thief, Eichkao, tried to steal away her little body, and great white Gavarushka tried to take away her eyes as playthings for his children. And

he slept a great deal on the rocks, letting the silken-haired ones come

"Gavarushka tried to take her eyes."

and go as they would, not caring where they were, or who might seize them. He went away from Tolstoi very early in the fall, long before the ground was white, and Kotik, who had been watching all the time from the rocks above, crept down and took his place.

Atagh swam out slowly around Tolstoi Head and across to the Great Reef. Then he turned to the north, to the soft resting place on Zoltoi

Sands, where he had often slept in the after-
noons when he was a bachelor. Then he crept
slowly out of the water, his broad feet sinking
deep in the shining sands. Then he shook
himself, and looked backward toward Tolstoi,
and groaned again over all the cares of life,
and the tears made wet strips across his
cheeks. Then he shuffled back over Zoltci
sands to the Great Dunes, where the sands lie
in smooth banks between tufts of tall rye-grass.
Here Atagh lay down and went to sleep.

And when Kotik came back in the spring
and climbed over the broken ice-floes to take
his place at Tolstoi, Atagh was sleeping yet.

And now the dreary days have come to the
twin Mist-Islands. The ships of the Pirate
Kings swarm in the Icy Sea. To the
islands of the Four Mountains they
have found the way. The great
Smoke-Island has ceased to roar,
because it cannot keep

"The decks of the schooners, smeared with their milk and their blood."

"The ships of the Pirate Kings."

them back. The blood of the silken-haired ones, thousand by thousand, stains the waves as they rise and fall. The decks of the schooners are smeared with their milk and their blood, while their little   ones are left on the rocks

"To the islands of the Four Mountains they have found their way."

to wail and starve. The cries of the little ones go up day and night from all the deserted homes, from Tolstoi and Zoltoi, from Lukanin and Vostochni, and from the sister island on Staraya Artil. Meanwhile, Kotik and Unga, Polsi and Holostiak, stand in their places, roaring and groaning, waiting for the silken-haired ones that never come.

Their call comes to me across the

" The dreary days have come."

green waves as I write. I turn my eyes away
from Tolstoi Head and put aside my pen. It
is growing very chill. The mist is rising from
the Salt Lagoon, and there is no brightness on
the Zoltoi sands.

Written on St. Paul,
The Pribilof Islands, Bering Sea,
July 28, 1896.

"Atagh was sleeping yet."

"The cries of the little ones go up day and night."

CALENDAR OF THE MIST-ISLANDS.

(Dates approximate and variable.)

Matka turns back from the Farallones, January 1.

Holostiak turns back from Cape Flattery, February 1.

Atagh leaves the Fairweather grounds, March 20.

Atagh passes Cape Cheerful, April 20.

Atagh reaches Tolstoi, May 1.

The beach-masters follow, May 15.

Arrival of Polsi, May 10.

Arrival of Holostiak, July 1.

Arrival of Matka, June 15.

Arrival of silken-haired ones, June 10 to July 20.

Height of responsibilities of life, July 10 to July 20.

Birth of Kotik, June 20.

Birth of majority of young, July 5.

Trampling of young in battle, June 20 to July 20.

The drives, July 1 to July 25.

Minda returns (yearling), August 1.

Kotik learns to swim, August 1.

Atagh grows hungry, sleepy, and gentle, August 5.

Atagh goes away to feed, August 10.

Polsi takes his place, August 10.

Atagh returns fat and lively, September 15.

The pirate ships enter the Icy Sea, August 1.

Lakutha starves to death on the rocks, August 15.

The Storm King drives the pirates from the Icy Sea, September 15.

Kotik is weaned, November 10.

The long swim begins, November 15.

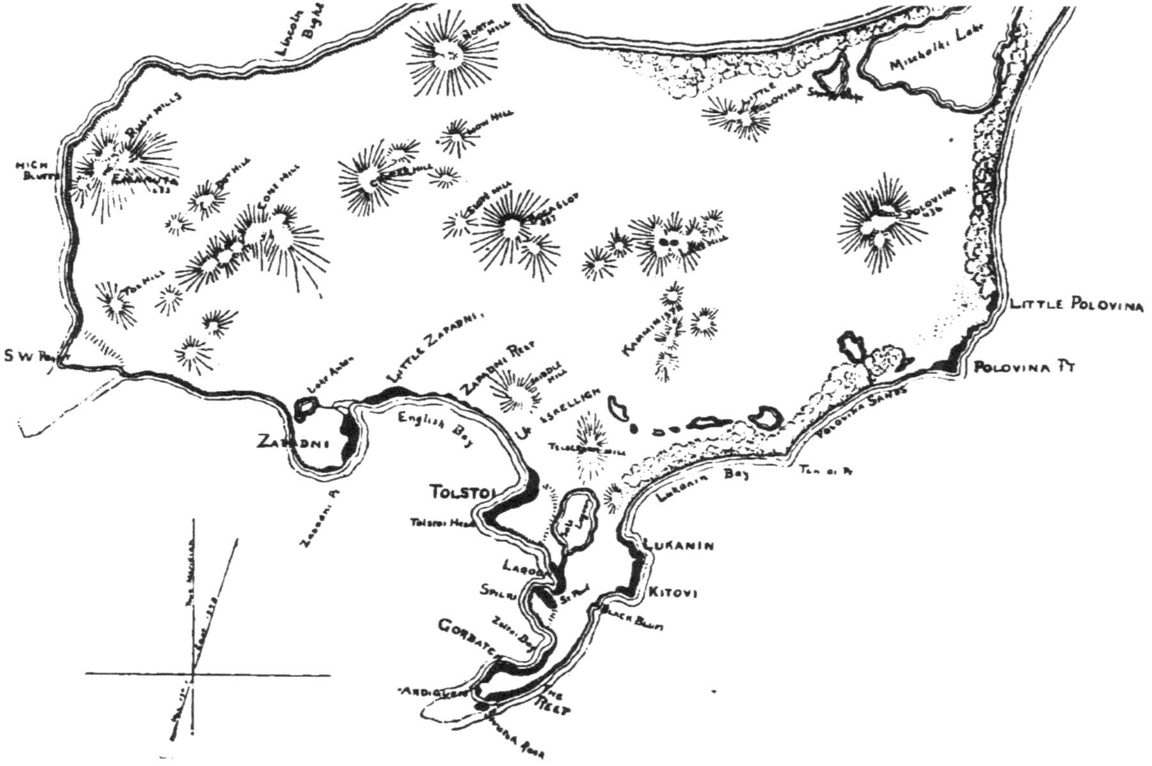
Lincoln Bight
North Hill
Mischelki Lake
Little Polovina
High Bluffs
Cone Hill
Polovina
Little Polovina
S W Point
Little Zapadni
Zapadni Reef
Polovina Pt
Zapadni
English Bay
Polovina Sands
Lukanin Bay
Tolstoi
Tolstoi Head
Lukanin
Lagoon
Kitovi
St Paul
Black Bluffs
Gorbatch
Reef

APPENDIX TO MATKA AND KOTIK.

❦

THE MIST ISLANDS AND THEIR NEIGHBORS.

St. Paul Island, the scene of the Story of Matka and Kotik, is one of a group of five rocky islands lying in the southeastern portion of Bering Sea, in Lat. 57 N. and Long. 170 W. This island and its companion, St. George, each about a township in area, are the only important ones in the group. The islands were first discovered by the Russian navigator Gerassim Pribilof in 1786 and bear his name today. In summer they are all but constantly enveloped in fog occasioned by the meeting of the warm Japan current with the icy current from the Arctic. Hence they are appropriately called the "Mist Islands." They are volcanic in origin, treeless and without possibilities of cultivation. Yet their plains are covered with wild flowers (p. 15) and their valleys with luxuriant grasses. In winter the skies are clear and the weather cold. Snow falls and late in the winter the drift ice from the Arctic packs (p. 50) in for a time about them. There are no harbors or safe anchorage against the storms of winter and the islands are therefore absolutely cut off from one another and from the rest of the world during the greater part of the year.

Cape Newenham on the mainland of Alaska is the nearest land to the eastward, three hundred miles away. To the south, two hundred miles distant, is Unalaska Island, in the Aleutian archipelago. This island contains the rugged old mountain Makushin (p. 53). It contains also the harbor of Unalaska, now familiar as a way-station for vessels bound for St. Michaels and the Yukon. The twin passes of Akutan and Unalaga separate Unalaska Island from Akutan Island, on which is the volcano (p. 52) of the same name. The next island to the eastward is the "Moss Island," Unimak, on which is the beautiful snow-clad cone of Shishaldin, (p. 52) rising nearly ten thousand feet in height. This is "where the Storm King has his kitchen." There are probably branch kitchens at Akutan and Makushin, for all three volcanos "steam and puff."

Near Unalaska Island, and between it and the Pribilof Islands are the "Twin Smoke Islands," Old and New Bogoslof. The first of these (p. 36) rose a red hot mountain peak from the sea in 1795. Beside it for a long time stood a single shaft of stone known as Sail Rock. This disappeared in 1883 and a second burning mountain (p. 64) rose from the sea to the accompaniment of subterranean thunders and earthquake shocks. This second island has now too ceased to "sputter day and night," though it is still warm.

The "Twin Storm Islands" (p. 58) lie at the other side of Bering Sea, near the coast of Kamchatka. These are the islands of Bering and Medni, the Komandorski, or islands of the Commander, so named in honor of their discoverer, Vitus Bering. While returning from his

momentous voyage of 1741, in which he found the mainland of the American continent in the vicinity of Mt. St.
Elias, his vessel was wrecked on the island which bears
his name, and there Bering and most of his company
died. The survivors escaped the following spring, taking
with them knowledge of the immense herds of fur-bear-
ing animals which made their homes on the new islands.
These islands are intimately connected in history with the
Pribilof Islands because it was the search for new island
homes and new herds of ''sea bears'' or fur seals that led
forty-five years later to Pribilof's discovery.

THE FUR SEALS AND THEIR NEIGHBORS.

The fur seals of the southern hemisphere are widely
scattered among the islands of the South Seas. Those
of the north are confined to the islands of the North
Pacific Ocean, and chiefly to the Pribilof and Commander
groups, with certain islands in the Kuril chain to the
north of Japan. We are indebted to Georg Wilhelm
Steller, a German naturalist connected with Bering's
expedition of 1741, for our first knowledge of the fur
seals of Bering Sea.

The hair seal, Isogh, and Sivutch, the sea lion, share
with the fur seals the shores of St. Paul and all three live
in neighborly relations. The hair seal (p. 25) is the true
seal. The fur seals are more properly what their discoverer called them, ''sea bears.'' The sea lion (p. 44)
of the Pribilofs is the same animal that makes its home on
Ano Nuevo Island and the Farallones and has made the
Seal Rocks of San Francisco famous. He was one of the
''four beasts of the sea'' which Steller studied in the
Commander Islands in 1741.

The sea otter (p. 37) Chignotto or Bobrik, a timid creature whose fur is now of exceeding great value, once lived in the kelp beds about the Pribilof Islands, particularly Otter Island, which has its name from this fact. The Russians called it "Bobrik." But Bobrik has abandoned these shores as well as most other haunts accessible to man, and his race is well nigh extinct.

Amogada, (p. 37) the Pacific Walrus, was once well known to the shores of St. Paul, and great areas on Morjovi beach are still covered with his bones. Until within very recent years a herd of three hundred or more of these beasts made Walrus Island, just off the shore of St. Paul, a summer resting place; but the sportsman's rifle has driven them back to their fastnesses in the Arctic. The picture of Amogada is taken from a mounted specimen, in the National Museum at Washington, captured on Walrus Island.

Eichkao, (p. 41) the blue fox, is and always has been an interesting inhabitant of the Pribilof Islands. Steller found him on the Commander Islands also, and Bering's men had difficulty in keeping their dead and dying comrades from his teeth. His "fox walks" today on St. Paul radiate in all directions, from his dens in the castle-like rock piles, to the cliffs where Epatka, the sea parrot (p. 63) and his associates the guilemots and chutchkis, (p. 17) have their nests. His long silken fur is scarcely less valuable than that of the fur seal itself.

There were no native people on the Pribilof Islands when found. This is a characteristic of islands occupied by the fur seals as breeding homes. The Russians, however, early in the present century brought over

Aleuts from Attu and Unalaska islands to work the fur
seal industry and the descendants of these now look upon
the islands as their home. They live in two very comfortable villages, the one on St. Paul numbering about two
hundred souls, that on St. George, about half as many.
Each village has its "company" store, its church of the
Greek-Russian faith and its English school. Agents of
the Government and agents of the Company leasing the
fur seal industry, care for the welfare of the Aleuts, for
the seals and the various interests involved.

THE NATURAL HISTORY OF THE FUR SEALS.

The animals spend only the summer on the islands.
The adult males land early in May (pp. 17 and 49) and
are followed in June and July by the females. Each
"beachmaster" (p. 18), in accordance with the polygamous
habit of the animals gets about him as many females as he
can control. These family groups are called "harems"
(p. 22). A group of harems, defined usually by the con-
figuration of the coast, is known as a "rookery" (p.51).
There are about fifteen of these rookeries covering about
eight miles of shore line. The young are born in June
and July. By the first of August the rigid discipline
of the harem system relaxes. The beachmasters, which
have fasted since their arrival, go away to feed and
during the rest of the summer the mothers come and
go between the fishing banks far out in Bering Sea and
their young on shore. The young learn to swim (p. 35)
at the age of six weeks and afterwards spend most of
their time in the water. In November, when the severe
storms of winter begin, mothers and young leave the

islands. The latter are soon left to their own resources and the former make a rapid and direct journey down through the Pacific Ocean to the latitude of Southern California, where they are found in and about Santa Barbara Channel early in December. The females journey slowly back along the coasts of California, Oregon, and Washington—gradually picking up the other classes of animals which do not go so far south, —past Vancouver Island, across the Gulf of Alaska, by Kadiak and the Shumagins and through the Aleutian passes to their island homes in Bering Sea, where they arrive in June. The adult males spend the winter in the Gulf of Alaska, on the Fairweather grounds, and return earlier to the islands.

THE FUR SEAL INDUSTRY.

Owing to the polygamous habit of the fur seals the greater part of the males born are superfluous. The principle of killing therefore, as worked out by the Russians and followed by our Government in its management of the fur seal industry, is to confining the killing to the young males of three years of age. These younger males herd by themselves (p. 54) at a distance from the breeding grounds. The Aleuts surround them while asleep at night and drive them up (p. 55) in great droves to "Asascardano" (p. 57), to be killed and skinned. The pelts, cured in salt, are shipped to San Francisco and thence to London to be dressed and dyed. From London they are distributed to furriers the world over to bemade into garments.

The Russian government managed its fur seal industry

through a corporation to which exclusive privileges were granted. When the fur seal islands, together with the territory of Alaska, came in 1867 into the control of the United States by treaty with Russia, our Government at once leased the industry to a commercial company, reserving to itself a royalty or tax on each skin taken. For twenty years one hundred thousand skins were taken annually and the tax, together with import duties on dressed skins brought back for consumption in the United States, yielded a revenue to our Government of about thirteen and one-half millions of dollars. The cost of the entire territory of Alaska was only seven million two hundred thousand dollars.

About the year 1889 the fur seal herd was found to be decreasing. In 1890 it was little more than one-half its normal size and the quota of skins fell to twenty thousand. Since that time the herd has steadily declined. There was in 1880 doubtless two million and a half of animals of all classes. Today there are probably not more than three hundred and fifty thousand.

PELAGIC SEALING.

The decline of the herd was due to the development of a rival sealing industry at sea (pp. 66 and 67). This had been carried on from the earliest times by the Indians of Cape Flattery and Vancouver Island. These Indians went out in their open canoes a day's journey and hunted with the spear stragglers from the herd as it passed northward on the spring migration. White man's ingenuity soon found a way to increase this irregular supply of sealskins. Schooners (p. 66) were employed to carry the Indians and their canoes out to the main body of the herd, to move with them day by day and to provide a refuge for them at night and in times of storm. The plan was marvellously successful. From two or three vessels in 1879 the fleet of the "Pirate Kings" (p. 67) grew to a maximum of 122, in 1892 each vessel carrying from five to twenty canoes and hunting crews. The field of its operations gradually extended over the whole migration route of the animals. The catch of skins rose from a few thousand a year to a maximum of one hundred and forty thousand.

The effect of land killing had been to keep the males at a low point. The killing at sea, necessarily indiscriminate, fell most heavily upon the females. The investigations of the Commission of 1896 proved that fully three-fourths of the animals taken at sea were of this class. With the mother seal, killed in the spring off the Northwest Coast, her unborn offspring died; in Bering Sea her death involved that of her dependent offspring on the rookeries by starvation. By actual count in the autumn of 1896 at least sixteen thousand young seals were found to have suffered the fate of little "Lakutha" (p. 64). It was to emphasize these facts that the story of Matka and Kotik was written.

THE FUR SEAL QUESTION.

The effect of pelagic sealing was foreseen from the first though not fully understood. While it was confined to the open waters of the Pacific Ocean no action seemed possible. But when the pelagic fleet entered Bering Sea, in 1886, and attacked the herd on its summer feeding grounds, the United States sent revenue cutters to warn the schooners out of Bering Sea and to seize and confiscate those persisting in taking seals. This action was based upon the right claimed by Russia in 1821 to seize and confiscate vessels caught killing seals in the waters of Bering Sea. Among the vessels seized by United States officers in 1887 (p. 66) were Canadian vessels. A diplomatic discussion with Great Britain followed which finally resulted in a Treaty of Arbitration, agreed upon in February, 1892, by which the questions of jurisdiction in Bering·Sea, claimed by the United States in the interests of her fur seal herd, were left to a court of arbitration for decision.

This Arbitration Tribunal met in Paris in the spring of 1893, reaching its decision in August of that year. The decision was adverse to the contention of the United States and, in accordance with the stipulations of the treaty covering this event, the Tribunal formulated a set of regulations governing pelagic sealing by which the two governments might jointly accomplish "the protection and preservation" of the fur seal herd when on the high seas.

These regulations followed the analogy of our common game laws. A close season in May, June, and July was established during which the mother seal might bring forth her young unmolested. This was supplemented by a protected zone of sixty miles radius about the islands in which she might feed in safety when pelagic sealing was resumed in August and September.

These regulations failed utterly of their purpose because the mother seals feed not within the protected area but far beyond it. Hence they were slaughtered

without mercy in August and September and their help-
less young died of starvation on the rookeries. The result
was most disastrous and the season of 1894, the first under the regulations, saw the largest catch in the history
of pelagic sealing and was consequently the most des-
tructive to the herd.

The failure of the regulations was at once apparent
and our Government made efforts to secure their imme-
diate reconsideration. To this Great Britain, standing
for the interests of the pelagic sealers, would not consent,
at least till the expiration of the five-year trial period. In
preparation for such reconsideration the two nations
agreed in 1896 to submit the whole question of seal life
to a new investigation. The investigations for the United
States were under the direction of President Jordan of
Stanford University, with associates from the Scientific
Bureaus at Washington. Professor Thompson of Dun-
dee, Scotland, with a number of associates, represented
Great Britain.

At the close of the investigations in November, 1897,
the two commissions, known as the Conference of Fur
Seal Experts, came together in Washington and after a
discussion of the results of their labors reached a substan-
tial agreement as to the facts in the case. These facts
had prior to this time been, for the most part, in dispute.
By the joint agreement pelagic sealing was designated
as the cause of the decline in the herd, and it was further
shown that pelagic sealing in any form was incompatible
with the protection and preservation of the herd.

Upon the basis of this agreement the fur seal question
passed into the hands of the Joint High Commission

which was called together at Quebec in September, 1898, to consider and act upon a number of questions, among them the fur seal question, at issue between the United States and Canada. There it has rested without result since. The tragedy of the "Mist Islands" was reenacted during the summers of 1898 and 1899 and for aught we can now see, it will be repeated in 1900.

GEORGE ARCHIBALD CLARK.

Secretary to Bering Sea Fur Seal Commission of 1896-97.

Stanford University,

March 31, 1900.

www.ingramcontent.com/pod-product-compliance
Lightning Source LLC
Chambersburg PA
CBHW020557270326
41927CB00006B/871